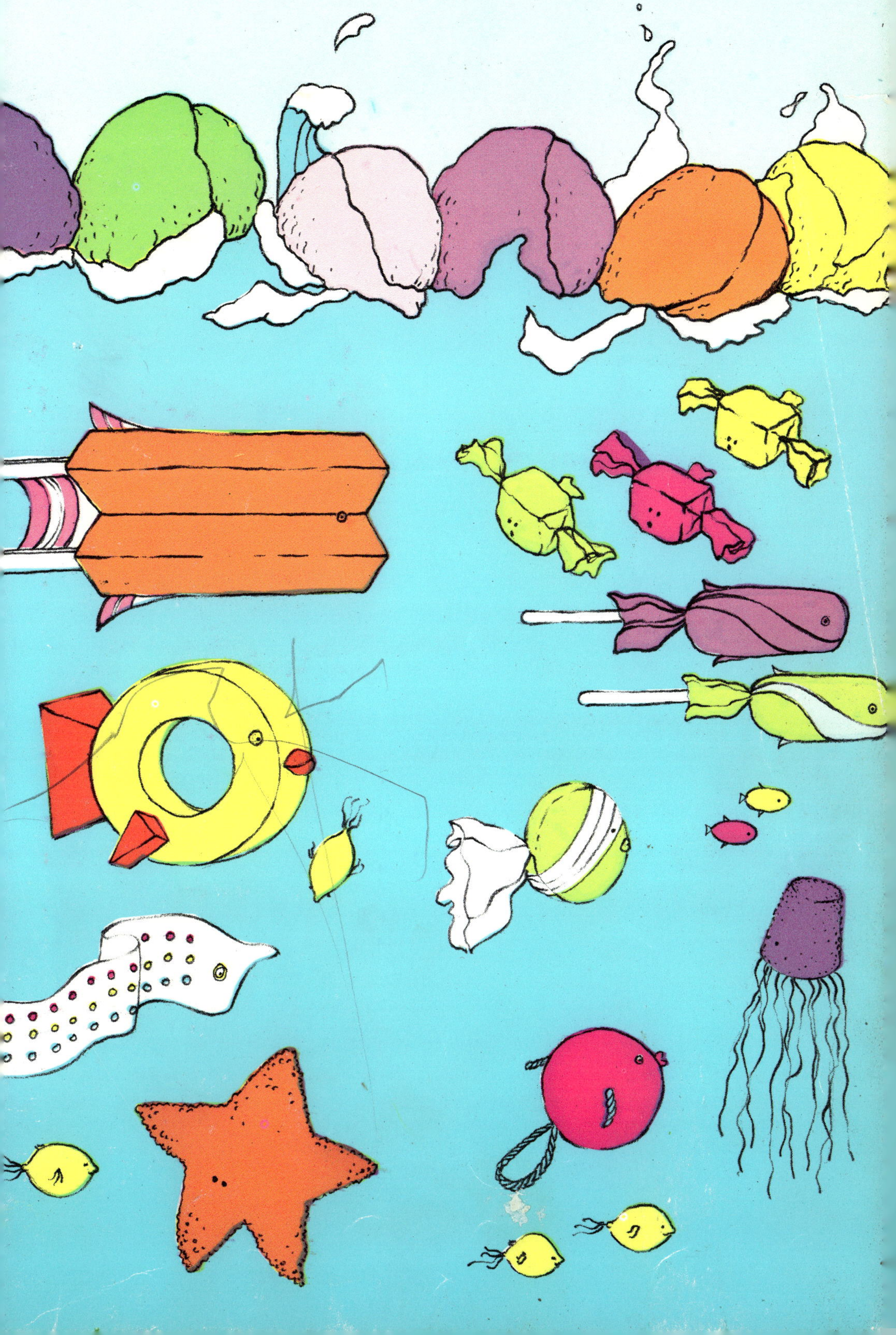

To Myrt and Leroy

THE ICE CREAM OCEAN

THE
ICE CREAM OCEAN
And Other Delectable Poems
of the Sea

SELECTED AND ILLUSTRATED BY
SUSAN RUSSO

Lothrop, Lee & Shepard Books
New York

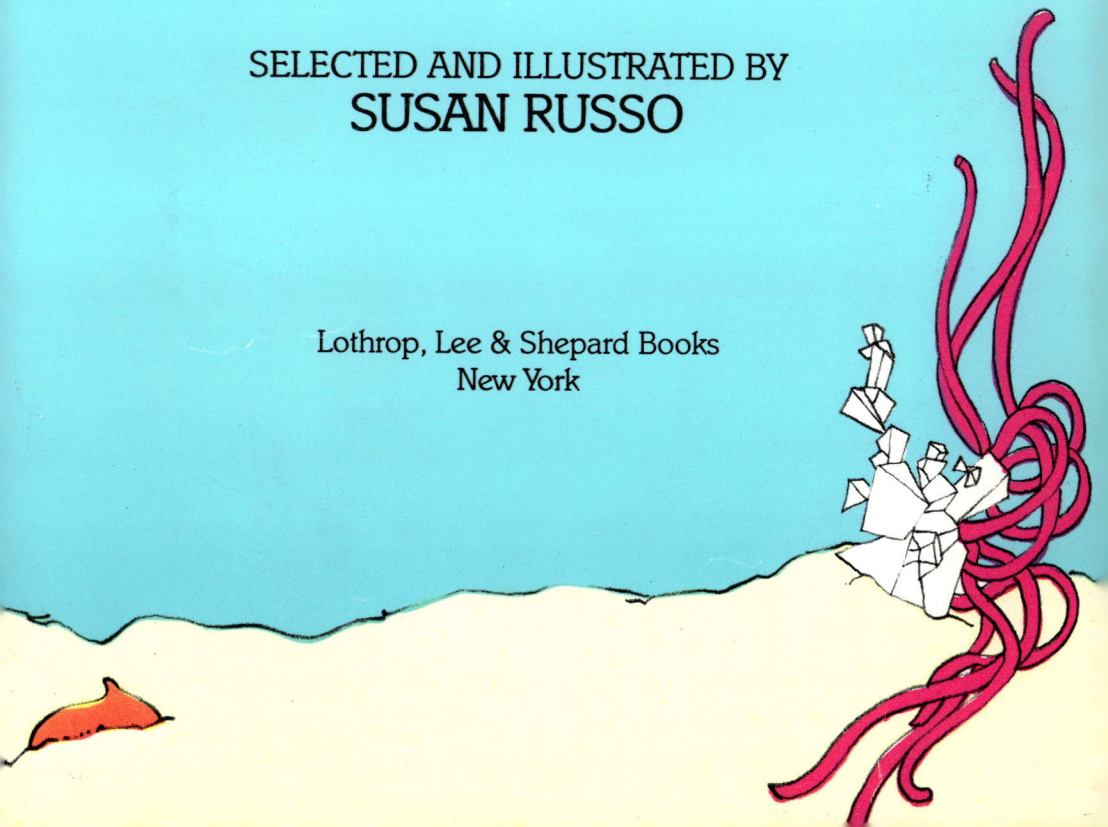

Contents

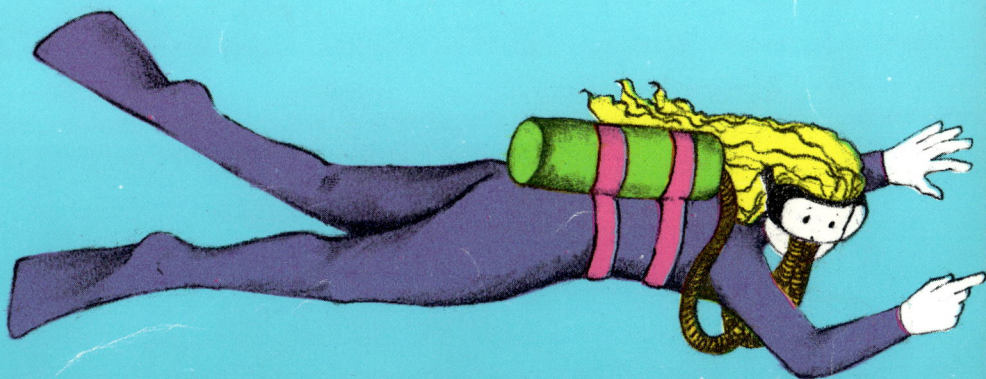

WHALE

When I swam underwater I saw a Blue Whale
Sharing the fish from his dinner pail,
   In an undersea park
   With two Turtles, a Shark,
An Eel, a Squid, and a giant Snail.

When dinner was over, I saw the Blue Whale
Pick up his guests in his dinner pail.
   And swim through the park
   With two Turtles, a Shark,
An Eel, a Squid, and a giant Snail.

William Jay Smith

7

THE ICE CREAM OCEAN

If the ocean waves could ever
    Be of ice cream made,
I could swim in them and never
    Be the least afraid.

If they made the finny fishes
    Out of lollypops
And the pebbles were delicious
    Little lemon drops,

If the sand were sugar candy
　　And the rocks were cake,
Just imagine what a dandy
　　Dinner that would make.

I would never more be lonely
　　With my pail and spade,
If the ocean waves could only
　　Be of ice cream made.

John Mackay Shaw

WHALE

A whale is stout about the middle,
He is stout about the ends,
& so is all his family
& so are all his friends.

He's pleased that he's enormous,
He's happy he weighs tons,
& so are all his daughters
& so are all his sons.

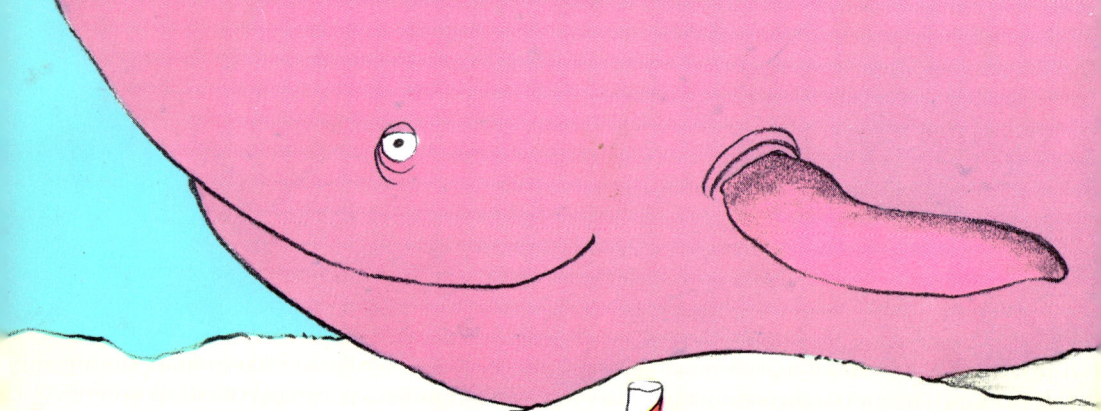

He eats when he is hungry
Each kind of food he wants,
& so do all his uncles
& so do all his aunts.

He doesn't mind his blubber,
He doesn't mind his creases,
& neither do his nephews
& neither do his nieces.

You may find him chubby,
You may find him fat,
But he would disagree with you:
He likes himself like that.

Mary Ann Hoberman

12

THE OCTOPUS

The octopus would surely be
The fastest pickpocket in the sea.
In a flash he gets all pockets done,
Instead of picking them one by one.

Sonja Delander

SEA HORSE AND SAWHORSE

A sea horse saw a sawhorse
On a seesaw meant for two.
"See here, sawhorse," said sea horse,
"May I seesaw with you?"

"I'll see, sea horse," said sawhorse.
"Right now I'm having fun
Seeing if I'll be seasick
On a seesaw meant for one."

X. J. Kennedy

15

A FISH WHO COULD NOT SWIM

There was a fish who could not swim,
A fact that sorely bothered him.

His father said, "Horatio,
I'll teach you how. You have to know."

His mother said, "I do not see
Why you can't swim as well as me.

"I mean, that is, as well as I.
Come on, Horatio. Please try."

Poor fish! He gave his tail a twist
And sank in mud up to his wrist.

"I can't," he said. "I can't be taught."
"You must!" they said. "You really ought."

They bought a book called <u>How to Fin</u>.
They asked the neighbor's children in

To demonstrate each Flip and Scup.
Horatio cried bubbles up.

"I won't!" he said. "I won't be taught!"
He threw away the book they'd bought.

"I want my lessons in a pool.
I'm going off to summer school."

He did. The teachers signed him up
For courses in Fin, Flip and Scup.

They gave his gills a friendly tweak
And had him swimming in a week.

The MORAL is: No child yet lives
Who can be taught by relatives.

Maxine W. Kumin

17

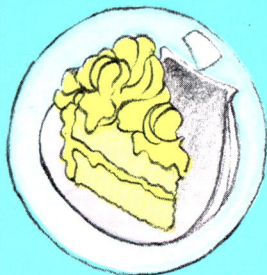

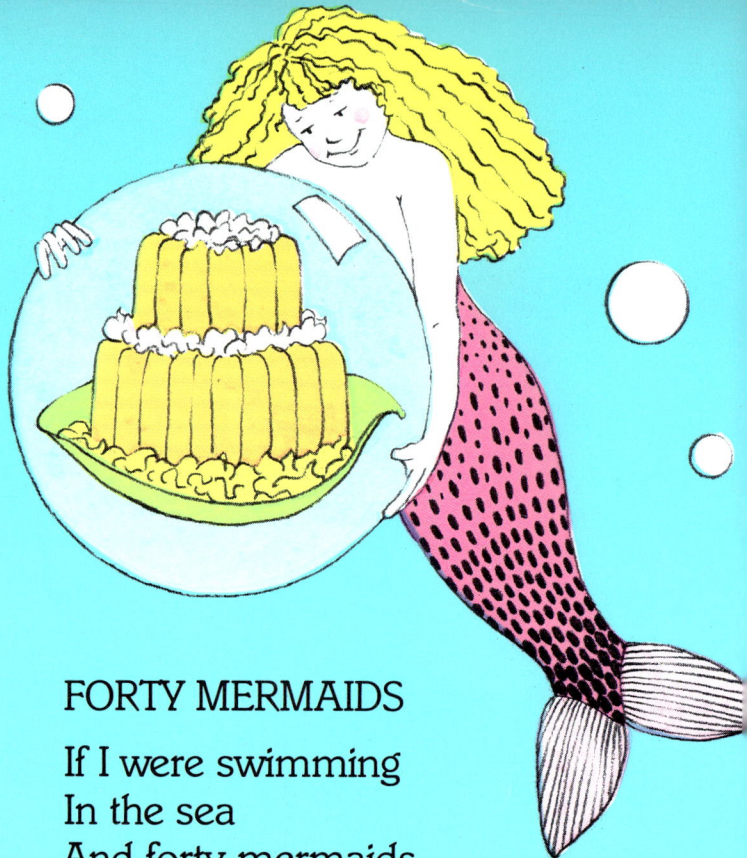

FORTY MERMAIDS

If I were swimming
In the sea
And forty mermaids
Came to me

And every mermaid
Wore a sign
Inviting me
To come and dine

With ocean heroes
Steeped in fame,
Like Captain Kidd
And What's-his-name,

And if the banquet
Hall were spread
With deep-sea ale
And ocean bread

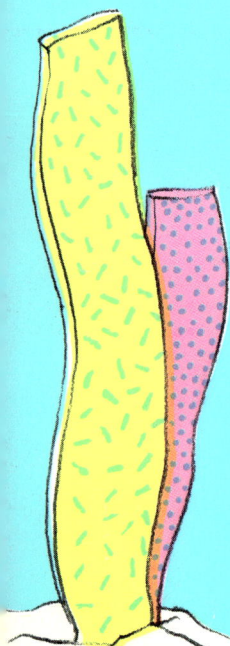

And all the plates
Were living shells
That floated by
On tidal swells

And waiters wore
Their fin and tails
And served us each
A pinch of snails

And then dessert
Arrived in bubbles
And everyone
Was having doubles,

I think I'd stay
An hour or two
Before I swam
Back home to you.

Dennis Lee

CAPTAIN KIDD
1650?-1701

This person in the gaudy clothes
Is worthy Captain Kidd.
They say he never buried gold
<u>I think, perhaps, he did.</u>

They say it's all a story that
His favorite little song
Was "Make these lubbers walk the plank!"
I think, perhaps, they're wrong.

They say he never pirated
Beneath the Skull-and-Bones.
He merely travelled for his health
And spoke in soothing tones.
In fact, you'll read in nearly all
The newer history books
That he was mild as cottage cheese
—But I don't like his looks!

Rosemary and Stephen Benét

21

I SAW A SHIP A-SAILING

I saw a ship a-sailing,
A-sailing on the sea;
And, oh, it was all laden
With pretty things for thee.
There were comfits in the cabin,
And apples in the hold;
The sails were made of satin,
The masts were made of gold.
The four-and-twenty sailors
That stood between the decks,
Were four-and-twenty white mice
With chains about their necks.
The Captain was a duck, a duck,
With a jacket on his back;
And when the ship began to move
The Captain said, "Quack, quack."

Old Rhyme

WARNING

The inside of a whirlpool
Is not a place to stop,
Or you'll find you reach the bottom
Before you reach the top.

John Ciardi

WHEN A JOLLY YOUNG FISHER

When a jolly young fisher named Fisher
Went fishing for fish in a fissure,
   A fish, with a grin,
   Pulled the fisherman in.
Now they're fishing the fissure for Fisher.

Author Unknown

25

There was an old man in a barge,
Whose nose was exceedingly large;
But in fishing by night, it supported a light,
Which helped that old man in a barge.

Edward Lear

26

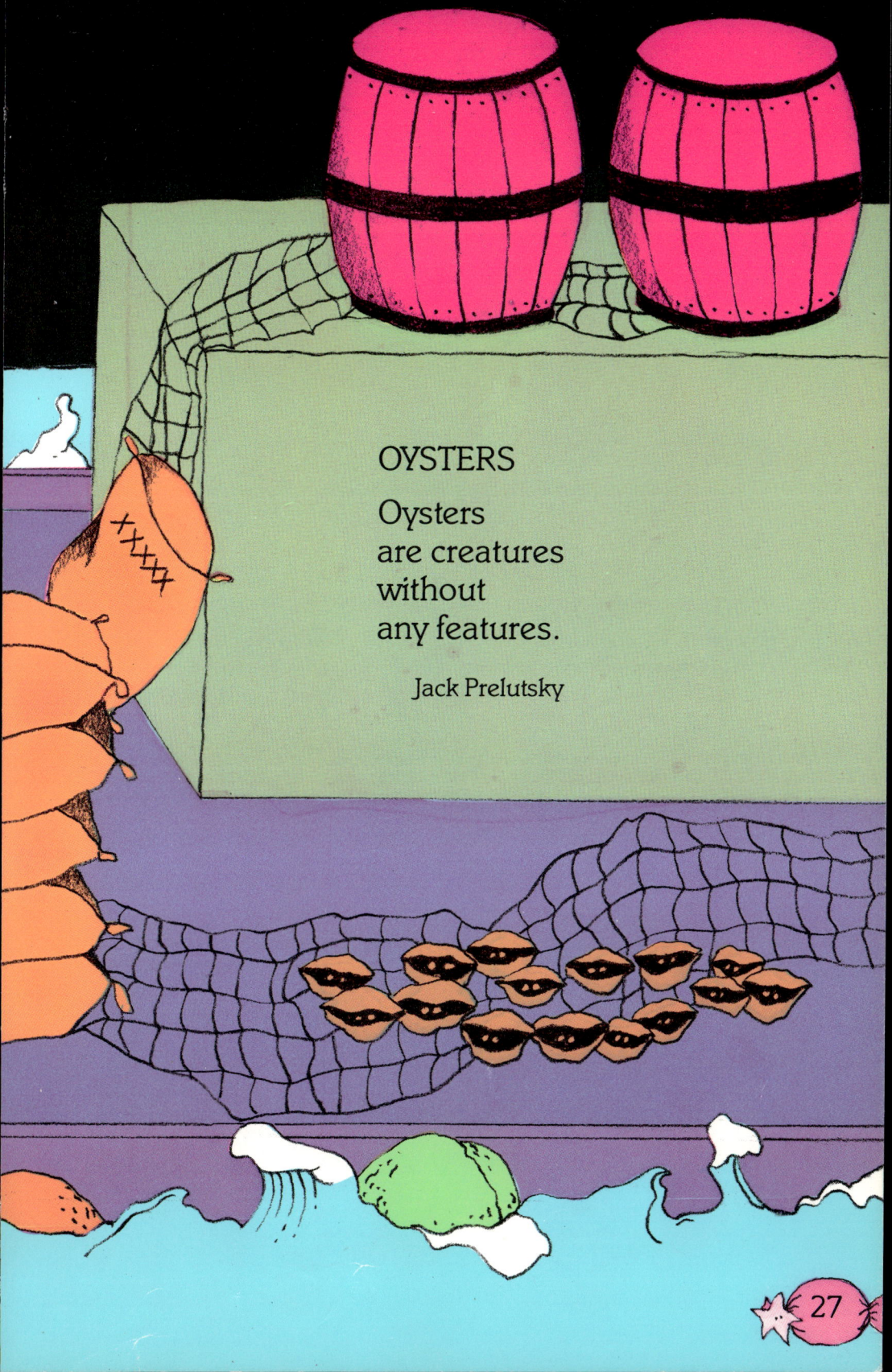

OYSTERS

Oysters
are creatures
without
any features.

Jack Prelutsky

27

Little Tee Wee
Went to sea
In a little boat
And while afloat
The little boat bended
And now the story's ended.

American Folk Rhyme

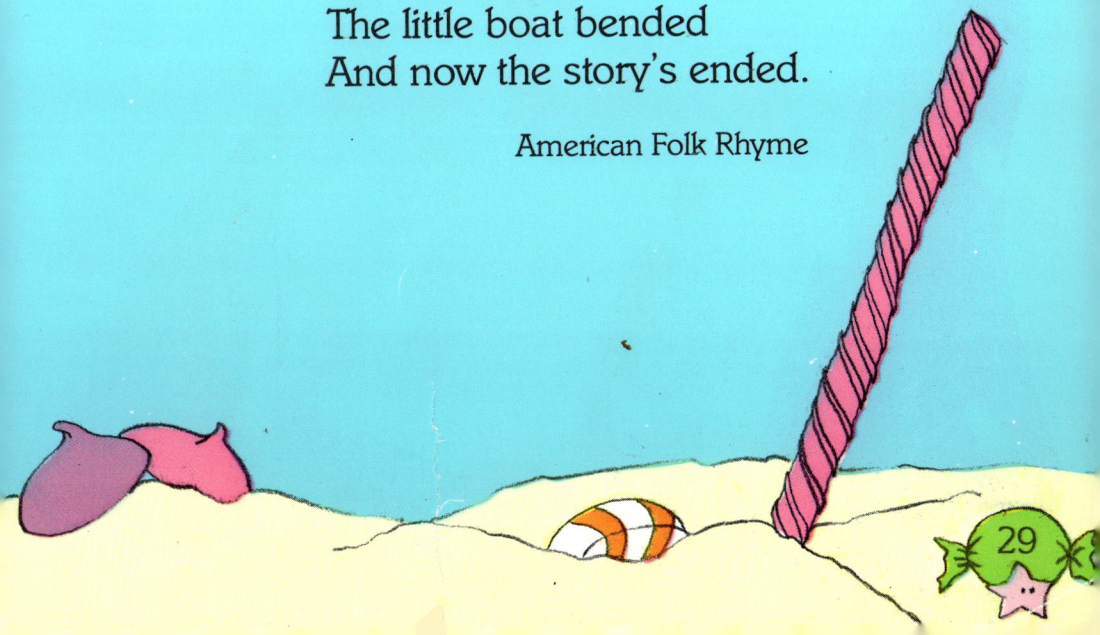

29

THE EEL

I don't mind eels
Except as meals.
And the way they feels.

Ogden Nash

THE JELLYFISH

Who wants my jellyfish?
I'm not sellyfish!

Ogden Nash

SEAL

See how he dives
  From the rocks with a zoom!
See how he darts
  Through his watery room
  Past crabs and eels
  And green seaweed,
  Past fluffs of sandy
  Minnow feed!
See how he swims
  With a swerve and a twist,
A flip of the flipper,
A flick of the wrist!
Quicksilver-quick,
Softer than spray,
Down he plunges
And sweeps away;
Before you can think,
Before you can utter
Words like "Dill pickle"
Or "Apple butter,"
Back up he swims
  Past Sting Ray and Shark,
Out with a zoom,
A whoop, a bark;
Before you can say
  Whatever you wish,
  He plops at your side
  With a mouthful of fish!

William Jay Smith

32

MERMAID'S MUSIC

Far out at sea the pretty mermaid
Plays upon her scales
To entertain the halibut
And lullabye the whales.

Her do-re-mis are beautiful
And liquid are her Cs.
She plays above the water
And below with equal ease.

But if she strikes a sour note
She stirs up mighty gales
And has to call a tuna fish
To come and tune her scales.

                              Jane Yolen

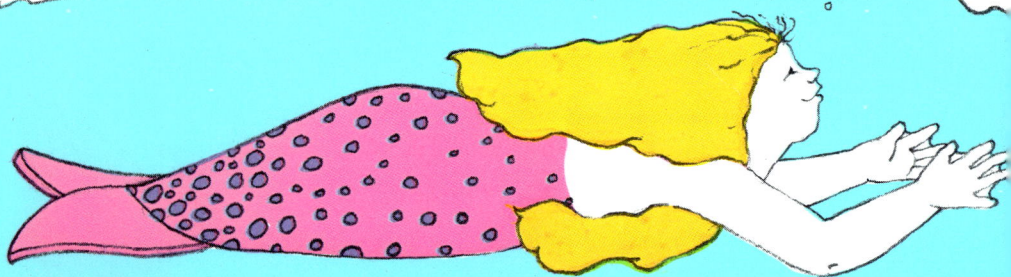

UNDERSEA

Beneath the waters
   Green and cool
The mermaids keep
   A swimming school.

The oysters trot;
   The lobsters prance;
The dolphins come
   To join the dance.

But the jellyfish
   Who are rather small,
Can't seem to learn
   The steps at all.

Marchette Chute

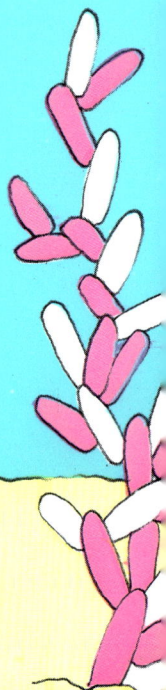

THE WHALES OFF WALES

With walloping tails, the whales off Wales
Whack waves to wicked whitecaps.
And while they snore on their watery floor,
They wear wet woolen nightcaps.

The whales! the whales! the whales off Wales,
They're always spouting fountains.
And as they glide through the tilting tide,
They move like melting mountains.

X. J. Kennedy

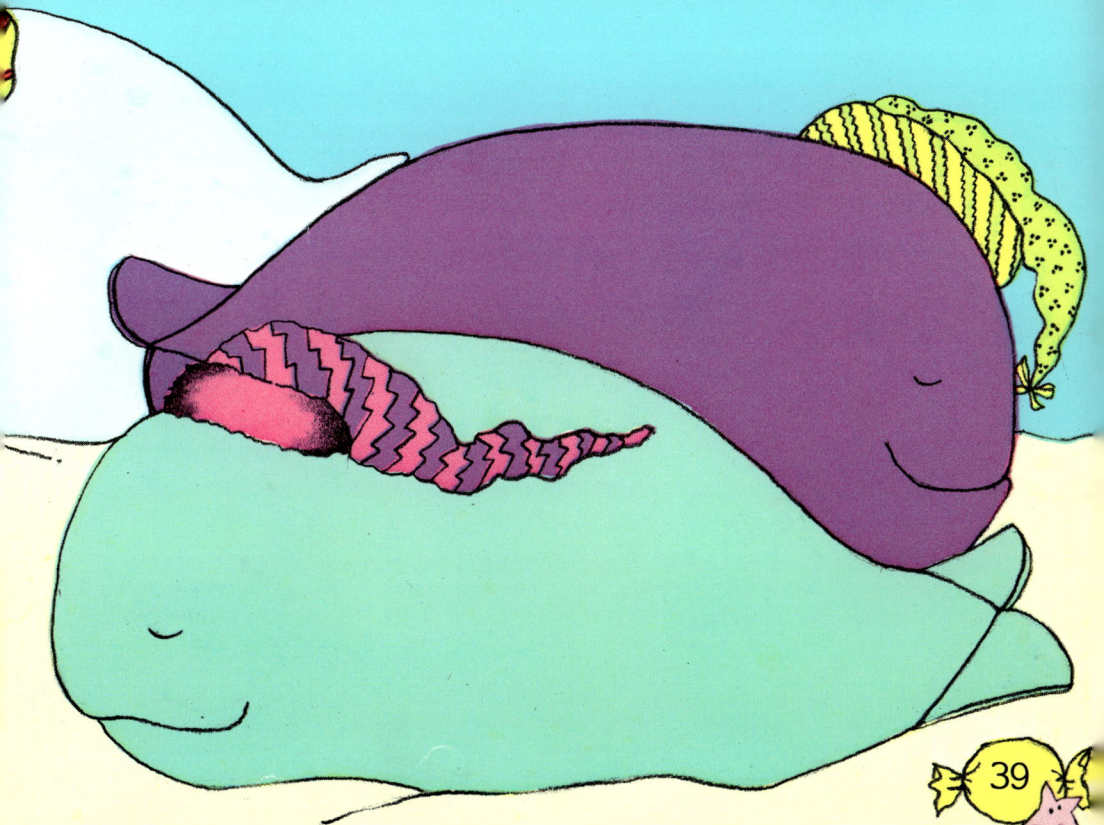

Permission to reprint copyrighted poems is gratefully acknowledged to the following: Atheneum Publishers, for "Sea Horse and Sawhorse" and "The Whales Off Wales" by X. J. Kennedy from One Winter Night in August and Other Nonsense Jingles. Copyright © 1975 by X. J. Kennedy. A Margaret K. McElderry Book (New York: Atheneum, 1975). Brandt & Brandt Literary Agents, Inc., for "Captain Kidd" by Stephen Vincent Benét from A Book of Americans by Rosemary and Stephen Vincent Benét published by Holt, Rinehart & Winston, Inc. Copyright, 1933 by Rosemary & Stephen Vincent Benét. Copyright renewed © 1961 by Rosemary Carr Benét. Marchette Chute, for "Undersea," which originally appeared in Child Life and is used with permission of the author. Curtis Brown, Ltd., for "The Eel" and "The Jellyfish" by Ogden Nash, Copyright © 1944, 1959 by Ogden Nash; "The Mermaid's Music" by Jane Yolen, Copyright © 1984 by Jane Yolen; "A Fish Who Could Not Swim" by Maxine W. Kumin from No One Writes a Letter to a Snail by Maxine Kumin, Copyright © 1962 by Maxine Kumin; and "The Whales Off Wales" and "Sea Horse and Sawhorse" by X. J. Kennedy, Copyright © 1975 by X. J. Kennedy. Delacorte Press/Seymour Lawrence, for "Whale" and "Seal," excerpted from the book Laughing Time by William Jay Smith. Copyright © 1953, 1955, 1956, 1957, 1959, 1968, 1974, 1977, 1980. The Friends of the Florida State University Library for "The Ice Cream Ocean" by John Mackay Shaw. Copyright © 1967 by The Friends of Florida State University Library. Houghton Mifflin Company, for "Forty Mermaids" by Dennis Lee from Nicholas Knock and Other People. Copyright © 1974 by Dennis Lee. J. B. Lippincott, Publishers, for "Warning" from The Man Who Sang the Sillies by John Ciardi. Copyright © 1961 by John Ciardi. Little, Brown and Company, for "The Eel" and "The Jellyfish" by Ogden Nash from Verses from 1929 On by Ogden Nash. Copyright 1942 by Ogden Nash. Macmillan of Canada, a division of Gage Publishing Limited, for "Forty Mermaids" by Dennis Lee from Nicholas Knock and Other People. Copyright © 1974 by Dennis Lee. Jack Prelutsky, for "Oysters" from Toucans Two and Other Poems by Jack Prelutsky. Copyright © 1967, 1970 by Jack Prelutsky. William Jay Smith, for "Whale" and "Seal," excerpted from the book Laughing Time by William Jay Smith. Copyright © 1953, 1955, 1956, 1957, 1959, 1968, 1974, 1977, 1980. Viking Penguin, Inc., for "Whale" by Mary Ann Hoberman from The Raucous Auk: A Menagerie of Poems by Mary Ann Hoberman, illustrated by Joseph Low. Text Copyright © 1973 by Mary Ann Hoberman. "Mermaid's Music" by Jane Yolen copyright © 1984 by Jane Yolen.

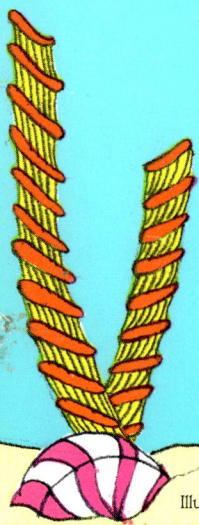

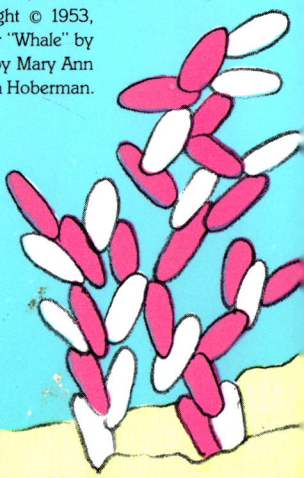

40

Printed in the United States of America.   First Edition   1 2 3 4 5 6 7 8 9 10

Library of Congress Cataloging in Publication Data

Main entry under title: The Ice cream ocean.

Summary: Humorous poems about the ocean from poets such as Ogden Nash, John Ciardi, and X. J. Kennedy.
1. Sea poetry.   2. Children's poetry, American.   3. American poetry—20th century.   [1. Ocean—Poetry.
2. Humorous poetry.   3. American poetry—Collections] I. Russo, Susan, ill.
PS595.S39I24   1984   811'.008'32162   83-16195   ISBN 0-688-02122-0   ISBN 0-688-02123-9 (lib. bdg.)

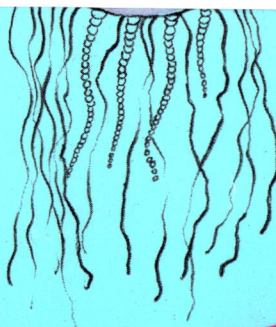

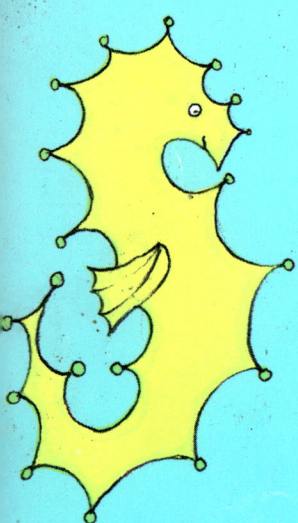

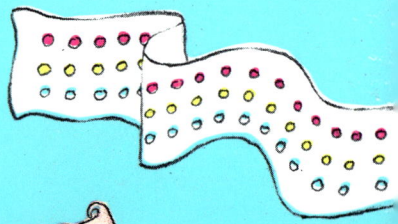

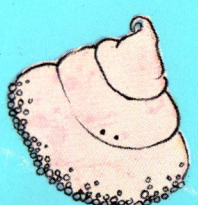

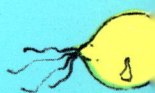